THE WOMAN'S JOURNEY

Stories of life, love & freedom

by Evelyn McAleer

The Woman's Journey

In memory of my Mother, you will always be the Rose
that reminds me of why I do what I do. x

EVELYN MCALEER

About Evelyn McAleer

Evelyn is a Spiritual Mentor & Inspirational Speaker from the beautiful county of Tyrone in Ireland. Evelyn works with clients on a one to one basis or as she refers to it, "walking with people on their journey." She speaks at many engagements, "2020 has been a blessing." I feel privileged to speak with people world wide through the gift of technology"

Evelyn's first two real life story books, "A Life You Want" and "Effortless" are available on Amazon in paperback and also on Audible and iTunes.

If you wish to avail of Evelyn's services, either for mentoring or speaking engagements, contact her through www.evelynmcaleer.com

CONTENTS

ACKNOWLEDGEMENTS

There are so many people who have helped make this book the little gem that it is. I want to thank all the women who have shared their stories within these pages. To my daughter, Erinrose, thank you for your constant support and for sharing your amazing talent in designing this book cover. You are on your very own woman's journey. You have shown courage and belief in stepping away from a job that was not your joy to create your own online business, erkmarketing.com, helping many people bring their dreams to reality. Thank you to the amazing Keelin Mc Gartland who edited this book, you are such a beautiful soul. Always remember that. Thank you to the men who have contributed to this book and for the time you gave to answer my many questions. Thank you to Declan Coyle and Jeffery C Olsen, to Jim Kerr, photographer and videographer and to Don Mc Gurgan, thank you for all your support and help behind the scenes. Thank you Catriona Corrigan, Divine Photography, for such a fun day doing the photo shoot and to my mystery woman on the front cover, thank you for your courage and trust in me. Thank you Andrea Clarke for the time you took to read my book and contribute with your foreword. Thank you CL for being part of my experiences and journey during the creation of The Woman's Journey.

Thanks to Steve and Don at the publishing company, I was truly blessed the day our paths crossed.

And finally, I want to thank a very special man, a man I owe so much to. A man that has always been with me, through thick and thin. He may not have understood what I wrote about, but he always supported me in any endeavour I chose to undertake in life. Thank you daddy (Nishy), who passed on 11 January 2021. You are now back in the loving arms of Mum, our Rose. I love you both with all my heart. I hope I continue to make you both proud and bring change to many lives through my books.

FOREWORD

As I start writing this foreword, I have no idea what is going to be revealed or what needs to be said, and I ask my angels, guides and the universe to help me, for the higher good of everyone who is led to Evelyn's new book.

When Evelyn sent me this book to read, I could resonate with so many of the stories of these amazing women. They have endured so much in their lives and have not been able to express themselves or speak their truth. Unfortunately, we as women have suffered for too long. We have been pushed aside and into the background, never allowed to stand in our own divine energy and power. However, with the help of Evelyn's amazing work and guidance, all the women in this book, myself included, have been able to move on and lead much more fulfilling lives, work through our traumas and be the best version of ourselves.

Evelyn is a truly wonderful and inspirational life coach who will take you by the hand and guide you to make positive changes in your life when you are ready. She will bring you light and help increase your vibrational energy, as she has done with me. My first encounter with Evelyn was only at the beginning of 2021 when her work was recommended to me by a good friend. I have followed the Law of Attraction for years and it is a big part of my life and work. However, Evelyn's words spoke differently to me. Evelyn breaks the law of attraction down into simple, understandable points. She makes it accessible to everyone and helps you to believe that anyone can use the Law of Attraction to create an amazing life. After listening to and reading Evelyn's books, I was inspired to reach out to her to study more and this is how we came to fully connect.

They say that everything in life happens for a reason and I believe Evelyn and I were meant to cross paths. We both have a story to tell and a strong desire to help and empower other women. So what I want to tell you is this....

Step into your power and take control, create the life you want and speak your truth with courage and integrity. Love yourself more than anyone else. Know it is never too late to change and don't look to the past or look too far ahead.

We are given each day as a present, treat it as a beautiful gift from God and make every day count. Live your best life, be happy, be love, be joy, be grateful and have fun!

Thanks to Evelyn for inspiring us with her wonderful books and touching our lives with her incredible passion in her own unique way. I am sure this is only the start of an amazing journey and she will continue to be a blessing to many others. The stories in this book are real, raw and incredibly encouraging to all women out there. A fantastic reminder that we have all we need within us and anyone can make a difference in their life by using the tools Evelyn shares.

Keep spreading your light and love wherever you go.

Andrea Clarke
Feet First Therapies & Training School

INTRODUCTION

Each and every person has a story to share and I believe in sharing we help many others. I did not know I would write a third book, in fact, I didn't know I would write a first book! It just happened at the right time and, as always, I trust that my steps in life will be guided with ease. It was during a coaching session with a wonderful client, when she told me of the changes she was beginning to see in her life. After her morning walk one Thursday, she came home, had her shower and put on her finest red underwear. I remember smiling and saying, "Go you, and it's only Thursday!" That's all it took for this book to be written. The title and image came soon after. I knew the right women would come along at the right time to share their journeys. And so it is. The Woman's Journey was born. You may resonate with what they have shared or you may think that none of them have gone through what you have. No matter the story, no matter the experience, no matter where you live, no matter your bank balance, no matter your religion or skin colour, feelings and emotions are felt and experienced by us all. The woman who has one million pounds in her bank account has the same feelings and emotions as the woman with one pound in her bank account. When we cannot fully accept and love ourselves for who we really are, what we own doesn't really matter. Our thoughts, words and actions will determine what is reflected back to us. Change can be as easy as rising early in the morning to go for a walk, but if you do nothing then nothing will be your end result.

We all have so much more in common than we believe and I witness this first hand through the ladies I work with. We fear other women will judge us, we believe we are not important, we believe we haven't achieved success and wonder what we have to offer. There is nothing dividing us, only the thoughts we tell ourselves.

The expression of our femininity has too long been defined by a masculine-oriented society. It's time for you to discover and express your feminine side, not the one that has been defined for you. Living in a fast-paced world has disconnected us from the concepts of:

- Receptivity and Presence
- Life as Sacred
- Loving Kindness
- Self-nurturing
- Allowing things to just "be"

Your divine feminine Goddess is that part of you that is wild, free and sensually expressive. It is that part of you that is uninhibited yet wiser than you can ever imagine. The part that stays emotionally centred and is not afraid to speak the truth. The divine feminine is powerful and she wants to be expressed, in male and female forms. Trust and honour that intuition.

I believe 2020 was a year that removed the fast pace for people who were unable to do it for themselves. It has been a year when so many women have awakened to that power within, almost like it was sitting in the shadows just waiting to be released.

THE REFLECTION

As I stood looking at my own reflection I heard, "Can you see me? Can you feel me? Can you hear me?" "Yes," I replied, "I can hear you." "But you can't see me and you can't feel me," the inner voice says. "You see me in everything outside of you. You see me in others. You know that I am within you, I am you, but you've never truly seen me. For if you did, you would have soared the high heavens. I know you feel me in meditation and in silence but you've never felt that feeling about YOU in your silence, you see me as separate. Sometimes you fear being alone or in silence with yourself. I AM LOVE. Fear is not of the divine. It is only when you come to truly see me within you, that I AM YOU, that you will break free. You will breathe, you will soar to heights of your own choosing. You ask many to see the magnificence within themselves, for that is what you see. I am you, I can only see magnificence, I have been here all this time waiting for you to awaken.

SEE ME
HEAR ME
FEEL ME."

Chapter 1 - The Underwear

She remembered a young girl full of zest, full of love for herself and life. She remembered that she didn't even know of any other existence other than fun and laughter. She remembered at the age of five when visitors came to her home, she pulled on a dress and a little bracelet she had from her christening. She knew if she stretched the bracelet out it would easily fit onto her wrist. She loved who she was, spinning around in her dress feeling like a princess, and she skipped down the stairs of the family home carefree and full of excitement to greet the guests.

She remembered when it all changed. The divine being that had come to this world was about to have her rebirth into the illusion of this 'real world' and others opinions. As her little feet touched the last step, her brother seven years her senior said, "Look at you, you think you are something special. Well let me tell you this, YOU AREN'T!" And that was the beginning of a not so pleasant way of life. As she grew older, relationships with men would affirm back to her the beliefs she held about herself, "You have fat wrists", "I'm telling you, this is for your own good!" "You've let yourself go, you've put on weight," a continuing stream of degrading remarks throughout her life. No matter how she dressed she always felt fat and ugly. She remembered asking a roommate at university, "Do you feel fat and ugly?" Her roommate replied, "I've felt fat but I've never felt ugly." Again she remembered what an astonishing answer, for she truly believed everyone must feel ugly.

Achievement after achievement, certificate after certificate, promotion after promotion, makeup, hairstyles, clothes.....she still felt fat and ugly. Until one day she remembered when she was five years old and the event that birthed her to others pains. She made the decision to awaken morning after morning and begin loving that girl again. She took herself out for a dawn walk and on her return she showered and put on her finest underwear, she done it all for her. She began to fall in love with her own company, she began to see the beautiful being she always was, she made the choice to make the change and all because she remembered to remember the divine I AM.

I AM LOVE

I AM LIGHT

I AM PERFECTION

I AM FREE

I AM ON THE COVER OF THIS BOOK

CHAPTER 2 - THE HIGH HEELS

A lady went to pay a substantial utility bill. This was a great day. Today she had money to lovingly give. She had built up her business, she received money by helping others, she felt it was the first time in a long time that she was financially stable.

"Today is a high heel day," she thought. She went to her cupboard, took out a pair of shoes she loved, placed them on her feet and drove to the local store to pay the bill. She stepped out of her car feeling like a millionaire and walked into the store as though she were walking down Hollywood Boulevard. In her mind she was ten feet tall, full of gratitude and love, with a smile for all to see. Today was a great day! After lovingly paying her bill she returned to her car repeating over and over again, "THANK YOU, THANK YOU, THANK YOU!"

This may be a very short story but this is love. Love of self, love for what she received, love for what she was able to lovingly give. Such gratitude in paying a utility bill, the effortless celebration and joy of it all. For it is in giving that we receive. So whatever you give today, should that be your time or your money, give it with love. If we begrudge our giving that is what will return to us.

She knew there would be plenty of days for the comfortable slippers but this was a day to pull out and put on the high heels.

How will you celebrate your day today? It's the simple things to celebrate you.

GO YOU!
YES GIRL, YOU DONE IT!

CHAPTER 3 - THE LOVE AFFAIR

The hope in sharing this story is that it may bring healing to your life as it has to the amazing woman who chose to confide in and trust me with her woman's journey.

Now in her fifties, she is reflecting on her journey which has taken her to a wonderful place in life and a place of peace within. Seeing the many joys, the excitement, the passion, the guilt, the tears, she has accepted all that ever was and now only sees the beauty this life has to offer and the beauty she always was.

At the age of nineteen she met a young man who became her husband in the following years. As she walked down the aisle, this was the man she loved, the man she would have her family with and the man she would grow old with. Life was good, he was the financial provider for the family. She was the mother, the wife, the caretaker for the home. She felt because she wasn't bringing in an income she would give everything she had to raising her family. A decent family, the children doing well at school, they all attended church, she attended school plays, school meetings, kept a good home, had meals ready and saw to everyone's needs. This she knew how to do effortlessly, no matter how tired she was or what she went without, she believed this was her duty as a good mother and wife. She was the only woman her husband had ever been intimate with, admittedly her own sexual experiences were pretty limited. Making love was another act of care for her husband, many times pretending she was enjoying the contact but seldom stimulated and never spoken about. She never brought it up in conversation because she never wanted to hurt her husband's feelings, in a way she believed it was serving a purpose - the creation of their children and satisfying her husband's needs. The thought of even talking about sex or how it could be spiced up was far too embarrassing, it is only now in her fifties that she can speak freely. Each day continued seeing to everyone's needs, all except her own. For if she did how wrong that would be? The feeling of guilt would have outweighed the feeling of deserving or self-love, in fact it would be selfish that she would even consider putting her needs before others. Settled and comfortable with the children coming first, there was no effort or time made for this husband or wife. Slowly growing apart in connection with who each other was, believing their connection through their offspring was enough.

It was a chance meeting the day she bumped into an old ex-boyfriend. When she last knew him he was a boy bridging on manhood, a boy she briefly dated, a boy she ended her relationship with to be with her now husband. Old memories came flooding back, days of youth. She remembered how he made her feel, he would have done anything for her. He had passion and in that meeting something sparked within her that she had long since forgotten. A flame lit within, she could see in his eyes he still had love for her. The excitement surged through her body, her heart raced, she felt alive. After chatting for a while he told her he was now married with his own family. The thought to have these feelings was so wrong, both married, both with families.

The sexual energy had ignited, youth was restored, the love affair began soon after.

So many emotions, the feelings of being desired, wanted, helped, loved, being seen as a beautiful woman, she felt wild, she felt free but along with that came the heavy burden of guilt, regret, sadness and total selfishness. The excitement of meeting each other helped with the mundane daily duties, it was a short escapism from being the mother, the wife, the caretaker, the upstanding church goer, it was a chance to be free.

It wasn't long before she made a terrifying discovery. She had fallen pregnant. Fear, panic, disgust, guilt and the shame of having to reveal this secret, knowing that her betrayal would be heard of far and wide. She and her husband had not been intimate for quite sometime, it would be evident the child was not his. Two families torn apart because of two people's desire to be loved, wanted and needed. She lost many people she thought were friends. She became paranoid, believing people were speaking about her. Should she overhear anyone talking about marriages breaking up or if there was a sermon in church on adultery, she felt it was always about her. A feeling she had let people down, the disgrace of having to tell her own mother, the disgust her children would hold within them towards her was a heavy burden to carry but she knew this was her punishment for her reckless behaviour.

When her child was born his father wanted them to be together. How could she do this to the children she already had? They hated him. His marriage had also ended. She reflected back to when they were teenagers, how overpowering and suffocating he had been but with the chance meeting, those memories never once came up. Now they were very much brought to the forefront of her mind. She felt she couldn't breathe and made the choice to just be with her children. An independent woman's pride took over. She kept up the front she had everything under control, never asking for help, the reoccurring thought, "You made your bed, lie in it!" kept the punishment, guilt and pride alive and well.

NOW, in her own words, "I give myself permission to let go of the past. I am living in the present. My past is part of me. I am thankful for my past because it has made me the person I am today. I am releasing guilt. From my love affair I received a beautiful child conceived from only love of two people.

I AM Loved

I AM Trusted

I AM Honest – especially with myself

There are many things we wish we could do or say differently about our past. If I had been honest with my husband about my needs, if I had asked him about his needs, I wonder would that have changed the course of life? It is not about the act of sex but the connection between two people. It is the connection of love of self. It is the connection to the divine source. I was afraid of hurting my husband and embarrassed to speak about sex but in the end I did end up hurting him. Be open with your partner, he probably will welcome any suggestions, try not to overthink what he will think of you. I still have a good relationship with both men, they are the fathers of my children. Today I love myself and in doing so I don't seek it from the outside. I never thought my connection with Evelyn would lead me on this journey. I never thought I would write about my story but such is the mystery of life, we meet many people for the growth of our souls.

I AM ALIVE

I AM IN A LOVE AFFAIR WITH ME

For I now realise I looked to the outside for approval that I was a good mother, that I was a good wife, approval that I was a good daughter, that I was loved, desired and approval that I was enough. The outside also had me believing I was a disappointment, that I was an adulterer. I look to the inside and see the perfect divine being I AM. I have always been loved for I AM of that love.

Chapter 4 - Love & Need

In this chapter I wish to bring your attention to the difference between love and need. I asked a group of ladies I work with to share how they chose to love themselves that day.

The true self will only speak to you with love, care, patience and support.

The Need

When we set ourselves goals, more often than not the doubts, negative thoughts and the needs creep in.

I need to eat less

I need to study more

I need to make time

I need to make an effort

I need to exercise

I need to meditate

I need to write

The list of needs is endless. The reason we need is because we have become attached to an outcome. We feel we need to do all these things in order to achieve our goal. Some of the goals might be to look thinner, to look more attractive, to get fitter, to finish or even start writing a book, to get more business, again the list is endless.

Drop the need/s, otherwise you will always be needing, never truly achieving or receiving a sense of fulfilment. What if you decided today to listen to the part of you which is love? I wonder how that conversation would go? Have you ever had a loving conversation with yourself? When was the last time you said something nice to yourself? Remember, if you want change, it must start with you.

Here are a few examples that I received from those ladies who decided to love themselves rather than needing to do anything.

I loved myself today to take myself on a coastal journey, to sit and have a beautiful cup of coffee and to take a long walk on the beach.

I loved myself today to awaken earlier and exercise my wonderful body on the treadmill.

I loved myself today to gift myself time before my children and husband wakened. I loved myself today to look at my beautiful face as I lovingly cleansed and moisturised my skin. I lovingly dressed myself and chose clothes that said "you are deserving of these beautiful colours."

I loved myself today to spend my morning giving gratitude for all that I AM. I loved myself today that I gifted myself the power of human touch with a massage. My body is deserving of relaxation, oils and gentle hands.

After reading these you may notice there are no needs. It takes a bit of practice to speak to ourselves in a loving manner, the usual habitual thoughts are mostly an array of negative needs, "I need to get out for a drive to blow off the cobwebs," "I need to get on the treadmill to become thinner," "I need to get up before everyone to get the house work done," "I need to get a massage to release all this tension."

We will continually focus on negativity when we need. We will continually attract into our lives that which we don't want when we need.

How will you finish this sentence for you?

I love myself today therefore I.........................

CHAPTER 5 - ALONE BUT NOT LONELY

Her friend messaged on a Sunday evening, "How was your day?" She replied, "I wakened early, had a beautiful bath full of bubbles, I treated myself to some tanning products, I dried and straightened my hair and I carefully selected a pretty dress for my wonderful day ahead. I put on my makeup and finally I sprayed myself with my favourite perfume. I was treated to the most beautiful meal at a very peaceful and tranquil establishment. I received the best service in all of the land, I had wonderful company and even treated myself to dessert and a glass of wine. Following all of that, I sat by the fire and there was even a movie playing. I removed my shoes and eased myself back into the cushioned seating. It was absolutely perfect!" "Oh my, that sounds divine,' her friend replied, "Where did you go?"

"I done it all in my own home by myself !" was the answer. "I dressed myself, I prepared myself for the day. I cooked for myself , I served myself, I was gentle with myself and all because I loved myself. If someone was to have taken me for dinner I would have dressed nicely for them, so why not dress nicely for me? I loved myself today to honour the great person I AM."

For many, they may find it difficult being by themselves or for those that have never known life without a partner or company, looking in on this story you may think how sad it is or perhaps feel pity. However, this is something I recommend everyone should try in their life, spend time by yourself. There is a difference between being alone and being lonely. I heard of a lady who was in a marriage for many years, a marriage she had not been happy in for a long time. She was afraid of leaving her marriage and stepping out on her own because the fear of being lonely haunted her. She realised after she 'stepped out' that her marriage was where she had felt the most loneliness . We believe that when we have company or a partner we will never be lonely. Believe me, you can be surrounded by one hundred people and still feel extremely lonely. You can walk on a beach, you can prepare a meal alone and feel the most alive you've ever been. It is one of the biggest fears a lot of people hold onto, that fear of being lonely. Never assume just because someone is in a restaurant by themselves or living by themselves that they are lonely. I certainly don't dispute the fact that many are lonely and find it very difficult in the evenings after returning home from work. They crave a loved one, someone to share time with, someone to share their love with. I believe if we show ourselves the best love we set the boundaries on how others should love us. If you treat yourself with kindness and care you won't accept anything less because you know you are deserving of only the greatest love. If you are 'between' relationships, please give yourself the space to fall back in love with you. If you seek a partner from a place of loneliness, it is not the vibration you wish to be on as you will attract that emotion back to you. I believe effortless love exists, I believe when two people can truly love themselves as individuals, regardless of what they have come through in their past, they are in a beautiful vibration to offer that love to each other without the expectation or need to receive it from the other.

CHAPTER 6 - A JOURNEY FROM SCREAMING TO HEALING

This chapter is in the words of Oonagh O'Keefe Co Clare Ireland.

I take a deep breath and close my eyes, I reconnect and go within, asking my angels for their assistance and guidance as I start to write. I ask that I only write from a loving space and that anything I am to say is only going to be of benefit to you. I can only speak from my own experiences growing up as a child in a family unit. As we are all on different journeys and I respect my family's privacy, their stories are not mine to share. These experiences have led me to where I am today, which is a very happy, peaceful loving space. I thank God that I am so peaceful now within my life. I promise, it is possible for you to find this type of peace too, once you are open to it.

I was born into a family where there was a lot of sexual, physical, emotional and verbal abuse. This was just part of my every day existence and I had never known anything different. I was brought up in a home where I saw many unsavoury things which no child should ever have to witness or be exposed to. My mother is a very beautiful, spiritual woman who carried many crosses in her lifetime and done her very best for us, her children. The love she tried so desperately hard to give and show us was overshadowed by such severe, fearful living conditions, but none the less, her love for us was infectious and when she was with us, we felt so safe and secure. My father, on the other hand, was a man who was a street angel, house devil as the saying goes. To the outside world he was groomed to perfection but he lived a life of lies and deceit. He carried around so much pain, hurt and anger within himself and he most certainly did not know what love was about or how to show it. The love he showed us was in the form of pain and anger. His way of releasing it was in the form of violence and abuse toward his most precious of cargo, his family. I was witness to this abuse in its many forms and quickly learned how to block out these visions and noises. Blocking out horrible experiences helps you pretend the world is just fine and all is well. It gives you a false sense of normality, even when you know deep

20

down that it is not the case. However, your body goes into a state of denial and you just keep going because if you do not pretend and you do not keep going, then what? Speaking your truth was frowned upon when I was growing up. If you came from a family where abuse was taking place, this was most definitely never spoken about. It was seen as bringing shame to your family's name and you may as well have handed yourself over to be shot if this type of secret ever got out. Moreover, when you came from a generational time like that of my mother and father's, well you can imagine, they never spoke about anything. To ask for help was admitting that you could not cope.

I was the youngest of three children, until my baby sister came along thirteen years later. I grew up in the '70s, at a time when there was no outside help or interventions for families who were going through any form of abuse like we were. There were no helpline numbers and phones were a scarce luxury. If you did get to make a call, you would have to cycle to the nearest phone box which in our case was three miles away. Trying to flee with your children as a mother or a father back then was not an option.

Staying where you were seemed an easier choice for most people.

Growing up in an abusive home affected me in so many ways. I became numb to life and started to develop many coping techniques, becoming a people pleaser being one of them, keeping the peace and staying quiet so as not to upset the house.

My abuse started when I was ten or eleven years of age. By the time I was thirteen, I had already grown up very fast, learning how to survive. My other option was to just run away and die. Which I did try to do. One day I grabbed my baby sister who was only very small. I took her in my arms and ran as fast as I could, just to get away from him. I wanted to protect my little sister and myself from my father's evil abuse as I could see he was starting to get a little more physical with her which really upset me. But like my mother, I decided to stay as I had nowhere to go and I was very afraid of the unknown. So even though it seemed to me to be an awful life, it was the best life that I knew of, so I put up with it as best I could. I lived in hope that each day the abuse would end but it didn't, not for a very long time. I had one thing going in my favour though. I always had a sense that someone was with me, a feeling of connection. This connection gave me hope each day and at times, it even brought me some fun. I could never explain where it came from, but it was something that felt very warm and peaceful to me. I would spend my days talking away to this source and allow myself to day dream. It was my form of escape from my reality.

I never got into this religion or mass stuff very much, even though my mother is a devout Catholic and made every effort to get us all to go to mass every Sunday. However, any time I did go, it gave me a sense of inner calmness and I did enjoy going to the Padre Pio missions when they came around every so often to our local church. I was always fascinated with how other people lived long ago and I loved listening to the many miracle stories of how people used to be healed in times gone by. Finding this spiritual connection brought me so much comfort as it helped me forget about my crap life. It felt like a reflection of myself that got me through my darkest of times. The older I got, the stronger the connection became and I started to visit my local church much more frequently. I would pop in on the way home from school to ask this God my mother prayed to for help. Even though He did not look in good shape himself, hanging from His cross so thin and bony, He was all that I had. On the days I was feeling very sad and lonely, I would stand and give out to Him and ask for help. After a while, I realised this connection was bringing me closer to something even stronger than myself. It became my best friend and gave me that inner peace and a sense that changes were on the way. It brought me hope.

One day in particular, I had to go to the doctor as I had a lot of pain in my stomach area and I thought, "Oh God, I am pregnant." That day I asked for help, more so than ever, as I really felt my world was about to end. I went to school even though I felt so unwell as school was my safe place. It was safer than staying at home. As I stared out the window from my desk, all I could hear was the teacher asking, "Are you with us today?" I was doing a lot of talking to my angels that day before my doctor's appointment. I was so fearful that my body ached from head to toe and I felt so sick. Sick with worry and sick that my mother would now find out. "Oh God, please help me," I begged. However, my father's dreaded words played over and over in my mind, "This is our little secret and if you tell your mother it will kill her and then I will have to leave you and you don't want that now do you?" he would say. It was almost too much to cope with, the thought that I could be the one who caused my mother to die.

I do believe my angels guided me to the doctors that day, giving me a pain so unbearable I had to get it seen to. When the doctor asked "Are you having intercourse?" I just wanted the ground to swallow me up. It was a day I will never forget. The doctor completed his examinations and to my great relief I wasn't pregnant but the pain I was experiencing needed further investigation. I fell to pieces and told him the whole truth of what I had been going through over years at the hands of my father. I begged him not to tell my mother and in those days, professionals such as doctors were not obligated to act on what had been told to them. He did get me some help from his wife who was a counsellor but it wasn't what I wanted which was a place where I could hide from my father. Now his secret was out what was going to happen to me? Was he going to kill me and worse still, would my mother find out and would she die?

What a mess. Fear took over my body and sickness crept in. From my asthma and eczema getting progressively worse, to not being able to eat to then binge eating. I told my father I thought I was pregnant, that I went to a doctor and if he did not stop I would tell. His answer to my cry was to give me a slap across the face. My world was over, I thought it couldn't get any worse, I just started to give up.

Despite bringing my story to the attention of authority, it was ignored and brushed under the carpet. So I just went back to being abused for many more years to follow. Fast forward to 1990 and after a very long journey of abuse, my father eventually served four years of a seven year prison sentence. I was also serving a sentence of a different kind. My abuse at the hands of my father ended but my self-destruction began. I lost my way, I lost the little glimmer of hope I thought I had found, I decided to abandon my angels and do it my way for a change. I did not know what love was and started to attract a lot of similar types of experiences and people into my life. I no longer believed in God or the angels and lost all connection to everything and everyone around me. After a very long journey and becoming a mother myself to two beautiful girls, I decided I had enough and my body screamed, "Please heal me and look after me. STOP doing what you are doing. Why ruin another generation? Why ruin yourself and leave your children without a mother?" This is all I could hear repeating over and over in my head. My marriage was in a mess and I had no intimate relationship worth talking about as to have an intimate relationship with another person, you have to be able to love yourself first which I had to learn to do. My self-destructive habits were starting to affect my children. I became so exhausted, I started to scream at the world, I started to scream at my kids and my drinking habits were getting worse and worse. Wine became my best friend as it took over from my angels and I drank every night. It helped me disappear from a world that was so painful to live in. When it got to the stage where I was starting to pass out on the sofa, I made a decision. No more secrets, no more lies and no more re-abusing my body . I started to reconnect and ask my angels for HELP ONCE MORE. They were still there waiting for me, ready for me to start my amazing healing journey.

My mother's words were more powerful than my father's words could ever be. They ring out stronger in my mind and have stayed with me until this very day, "We all need to believe in something to get us through this life. If you don't have faith in something, what else do you have?" Little did I know back then how powerful her words would become. I have no doubt that my angels are holding my hand each day, guiding me on my path towards even more love for my life. As I write this, I feel nothing but pure love for my father. I see him as a person who was never shown any love himself while he was growing up as a child, so pain and fear were the only path he knew. I thank God every day that we now live in a time where we can talk openly and get help, that our secrets do not have to be kept secrets and most importantly, we are heard and believed. Our mistakes are not mistakes, they are lessons, as we are all human beings doing our best in the time we are living in. I wish for you the reader, to be able to see only good come from this little girl's story of her life's journey and to see it as a lesson in learning how to love yourself unconditionally. Each and every part of yourself. The day I started to love who I was, was one of the best days of my life, apart from having my two children and meeting my husband. My family mean everything to me and I just want to be there as a light, to show them that love can replace any darkness within your life. I ask you to never turn off your light, to always believe, to always have HOPE.

A mantra for you to say:

I look in the mirror and I can only see a beautiful light that surrounds me.

I look in the mirror and I can only see a beautiful reflection staring back at me.

I look in the mirror and I can see a beautiful feeling of love and hope that pours over me.

I look in the mirror and I can only see a beautiful person staring back at me.

Who is this person?

Well, it is me.

Chapter 7 - When She Stopped Chasing the Dream, She Became the Dream

The source of a true smile is in an awakened mind –
Thich Nhat Hanh

Can you imagine as a young child being removed from your family home? Perhaps some can but for the majority it is unimaginable. Can you imagine as a young child being served dinner when it should have been your breakfast before going off to school, surrounded by destruction, turmoil and fear? Can you imagine not feeling loved when you were a child?

I can tell you that this woman is one of the most inspirational and loving people I know. I have often found that those people I have worked with or spoken to who have experienced childhood trauma have lost their smile. Who would blame them? What could there be to smile about? It was almost as if their smiles had been robbed or torn from them during their childhood and seldom found in adulthood. I'm not saying that everyone who has experienced trauma doesn't know how to smile, it is only my opinion and what I have witnessed from time to time. The exception is this particular lady, she has a smile that would light up any room. I could see the child within, she still had her child-like qualities. Laughter, joy, curiosity and imagination, it was all still very much present.

As she silently sat in reflection, the sun arose to greet her and welcome her to another day of magnificence. She felt calm, peace and so much gratitude, with tears of love for the life she now sees differently, for the woman she has become, for the belief in who she is, for connection to that universal source of infinite possibilities, for her connection to her God within. In a total state of bliss and gratitude for she is one with all.

So how did life change? There were many life lessons and growth in her thirty three years on this earthly plane. She once said, "Your heart will always keep tapping at you until you finally get it, what your purpose is and what your truth is."

Chasing the dream, not really knowing what she could do, drifting from one idea to another, investing money in one program to another, surely one of these investments will bring the dream, right? There is no holding back that power within you when the journey begins to becoming the dream rather than chasing the dream. All it takes is change and watch what starts to unfold.

In her own words......

"As I sit here this beautiful morning, it is day five of arising early. I am in my pyjamas in my kitchen whilst the rest of the family sleeps. I have the back door ajar, a coffee in my hand and the biggest smile on my face. The sun is smiling back at me, the birds searching for their breakfast. I am in awe of the brilliant beauty of the morning. Oh why did I miss this all these years? I place my two hands over my heart space, gently close my eyes and breathe deeply. Thank you, I say over and over.

I AM so grateful

I AM humbled

I AM supported

I AM connected

I AM guided

I AM loved

I AM magnificent

With tears in my eyes. it is the first time I have truly experienced the mystical calm of the morning. I am being present, immersed into all of its glory. I AM Blessed, I AM Becoming."

When we experience connection to the greatness within us and connect with the greatest energy ever, it is very powerful and emotional. It is a feeling of I AM HERE, I AM YOURS, I have always been yours. Change is not easy but the belief in yourself, in why you are here, perhaps not fully understanding the total 'why' but just experiencing what you know to be true in the NOW, that is what will pull you through each day.

No one had ever shown her true love and if they tried she would push it away, simply because it was alien to her, a belief perhaps that nothing good ever lasts or I don't deserve this love. She has come through the darkness, she is the brightest shining star, she is a mother, a wife, a daughter, a sister. She is the great I AM. She is inspiring many through her public talks, through her laughter, through her smile and through her tears. She is an angel delivered to this earth, bringing hope to all as she continues on her wonderful journey of growth, learning and love.

It all began with one thought, "I want to bring change to my life."

CHAPTER 8 - CONNECTION WITH SELF & COMMUNICATION IN RELATIONSHIPS

When speaking about 'The Sound Of Silence' in an interview, Paul Simon observed, "We have people unable to touch other people, unable to love other people. The song is about the inability to communicate." How true those words are for many relationships. When we lose the ability to communicate effectively, we lose all connection. Sometimes we believe we are communicating but the other person does not hear us or understand us. Sometimes, both parties want to be heard but neither is listening, ultimately leading to frustration and arguments. How frustrating it is, the want to be heard, the need for the other person to understand what we are trying to say. The hurt we are feeling, the old pain that needs healed, the explanation for an unanswered question that we try to forget but somehow always manages to creep back into our mind, all we want is for our mind to be put at ease. The fear of asking or discussing something, the fear of what the other may think when you ask. When is the right time? What will I say? Should I put it to the back of my mind? I don't believe it is ever our intention to insult or humiliate someone we care deeply about, but then again we can't be responsible for how the other person chooses to feel about, or react to, a certain topic or question. It may trigger something within them, it may send them into defence mode, it may cause them to totally shut off, pull the shutters down so to speak, as a form of protection from invasion or hurt.

So how do we communicate in a way that helps the other person understand where we are coming from? If you are feeling angry, frustrated, defensive or victimised, perhaps that is not the ideal time to communicate as you will possibly receive the same in return which will cause you to spiral further into that feeling.

As a dear and trusted friend shared with me after reading the beginning of this chapter, "What must be included is connection to one self. For if we cannot connect to ourself, it is not possible to fully connect with anyone else and if we cannot love ourself, it is not possible to love anyone else." For it is giving that we receive. What is it that you wish to receive? You must give without conditions and give freely in order to receive. If you communicate and give only anger then by all of the universal laws you must receive the same in return. The beauty of universal energy being that you normally receive more than you had even dreamt of. Imagine if you could communicate with love. Imagine the abundance of love you would have returned onto you. Imagine if you could speak your truth through love and have the ability to explain how you were feeling without either party getting angry or defensive. Is that possible? When we are not connected with ourself, we cannot fully connect with our partner. Communication breaks down, frustration builds up, thoughts spin around in our minds from past events, he said she said. Everything is energy, we are energy, our thoughts, words, feelings, actions, they are all energy. Sex is energy and shared with someone you are fully connected with in mind, body and spirit, it is the most powerful energy of all. Certainly there is sex where both bodies are together but there is no connection of mind or soul. A quick release of pent up hormones, an urge to get the business done, no time for fully engaging or perhaps no desire to fully engage because it's 'just sex'. Some have a desire to be desired or wanted, and feel sex is a way to show that. I have heard from women that their partners have said sex is the only way they know how to show love, but the partner assumes they are randy and it's the sex they want and not really them. Some have sex with their partners out of obligation or duty and not enjoying the experience themselves. I can't speak for all countries but I know for certain on the Emerald Isle, sex is not a topic that a lot of partners discuss with one another. What would they think of me if I suggested something? Is he going to ask for it tonight? Is she going to refuse me again?

Breath is the God Divine energy, laughter is the God Divine energy, children at play are the God Divine energy, it is the purest of pure. When you are told something is impure, thoughts or impure actions are sinful or dirty, that's when the purity dissolves and becomes only the word or the act. Physical and non-physical source energy expresses itself in physical form, you came forth to live joy.

Do you feel joy in your existence? There could be a variety of answers.

- I've never really thought about feeling joy.
- Depends on the day and what's happening.
- If work goes well.
- Not every day is a joyous day.
- There's not much to feel joyful about.
- If you saw the life I had you would understand why I don't feel joy.

Or,

- I find joy most days.
- I find joy in any situation.
- I AM Joy.

Sex has been here from the beginning of time and will be here until the end of time. I watched an interview with Esther Hicks who channels Abraham. The question of sex arose, Abraham answered, "We make too much of this being physical. We make too much of that which is non-physical."

(Non physical – not relating to, or concerning, the body.)

Hands up if you have ever had sexual relations that went beyond the body to the non-physical. I'm not speaking about zoning out wishing you were somewhere else, or with someone else (mind you,

I'm sure that happens quite a bit.) I'm talking about that divine connection to self, the non-physical that surges throughout your body, *energy, source, God,* that which we are all of. When you are fully connected to that which you are of, and fully connected to the one you share space with, whether it be the physical act of talking, laughing, working or sex, that is where the magic lies. That is ultimate oneness.

I asked ten men, varying in age and nationality, a few questions regarding sexual relationships so that I may provide balance to this chapter and hopefully deliver a better understanding of how men view this topic.

Question: **If you had some advice to offer women in regards to men what would it be? (I loved this reply from a gentleman who is very much connected in oneness.)**

My only coaching: Be whole, 100%, wanting nothing entering into a relationship. It is NOT a 50% / 50% proposition, but a 100% +1 and 100% +1 endeavour. 100 + 100 = 200, and with a little extra (+1) from each party, you may hit 212.

212 degrees Fahrenheit is where water boils, where things get 'hot enough' to boil and literally transform from water to vapour. That's when things get steamy. That's when relationships are meaningful, when each party says, I AM complete with or without you, but CHOOSE to offer my 'whole' (or holy) self to you in love, with no expectations, judgments or comparisons. Be 'whole,' individually and together, stepping into a new way of being 'unconditionally loving' beyond sex, beyond commitment and into the bold world of trust and oneness.

This line in particular stood out to me, "when each party says I AM complete with or without you." Such powerful words. Words spoken from the heart and life experience. This gentleman has come through horrendous experiences in his life, he lost a wife and child, he lost part of his body but from his pain he came to know 'oneness'. He experienced what a lot of us would never want to experience; please let his experience be enough for you. *To be complete with or without you.* What he came to know was the truth of his existence, he came to know completion within himself, he came to know that divine love which he was born of, he connected to love within. He remembered who he was. I AM perfection, I AM love, I AM compassion, I AM complete, therefore he did not seek it in anything or anyone outside of his existence, he was complete with or without. "I CHOOSE to offer my 'whole' (or holy) self to you in love, with no expectations, judgments or comparisons." Can you imagine being able to offer your whole self with no expectations, judgments or comparisons, either on yourself or your partner? No needing to be desired or wanted, but to just be at that place of full presence, of peace, of connection, of oneness. We need the body in order for the non-physical to express itself. However, when we remove focus from the physical and focus on the non- physical, this is where you reach boiling point, this is where you shift from the human form to just BEing.

Here is a little tester if you feel like trying it out with your partner. If it's more connection that you wish to bring into your relationship, having no attachment to physical sex, try and just BE in oneness with them. You may be nervous to suggest it, you may ask what the point in doing it is, but perhaps be willing to try.

Switch all mobile devices off, you don't want any interruptions. Don't get distracted by chores you have to do around the house or emails you have to send, they can wait. The most important people here and now is you and your partner. Use your living area, stay out of the bedroom. You can have a little relaxing music in the background, preferably no lyrics, the last thing you want is getting distracted by singing the song in your head. Have your room comfortable, with heat and soft lighting, the 200 watt bulbs might require sun glasses. You have to get naked for this one (I can hear the replies to that suggestion in my head). HOWEVER, if you are terrified some of the children or your mother-in-law might come through the door or wonder why its barricaded with the sofa and the pair of you are sitting naked, perhaps wait until a time when the house will have less footfall, or begin this experience with your clothes on and then progress to the full Monty another time. Like I said, there is no attachment to physical sex, though in some cases, when you get naked it may mean sex to your partner. This experience is about connection, it's about connecting to your partner in a way you may never have connected with him/her before. It is going beyond the physical form. So let's begin.

Sit comfortably opposite your partner.

Place your left hand on their heart and have them do the same with you.

If possible, when your partner breathes out, you breathe in and vice versa. The idea is to have one breath. Again don't get distracted by this, it could take a bit of practice, this time is about connection. If the breath work is not happening, just continue your normal breathing and allow your partner the same. Keep your eyes focused on each other. Direct eye contact. Just BE. No judgement, no comparisons, no speaking or expectations from either yourself or your partner. Allow yourself the freedom within to explore this time.

To reassure women who may feel uncomfortable in their own skin, one of the questions I asked the men was, "When you are intimate with a woman, do you notice what she believes are her flaws or insecurities i.e stretch marks, weight, lines, scars?" Each man replied NO.

So let's get back to the connection.

Have no time limit on how long you will be present with one another, just be willing to sit long enough to fight past all of those egoic thoughts that come in. If you choose to make love following on from this, take your time. Heighten your senses, feel the touch, feel the connection, and try to keep your eye contact. Have no attachment on the desired outcome of orgasm, just enjoy the Being of NOW. Do you remember when you were a child and were treated to an ice cream? You probably wanted it to last forever, you took your time to enjoy every second of it, there was no rush. Think of making love the same way. It's all in the journey and yes, the destination is very lovely but be patient, you will arrive there in divine time.

Have you connected with yourself today? Have you taken time this morning to give thanks for all that you are? Have you given thanks for your amazing body? If you are waiting for perfection in order to give thanks, know that you are perfect, give thanks now. Do you fully realise what your body does for you each day? The list is endless. May I remind you of your greatness. Your feet have walked hundreds of miles, your heart keeps life flowing throughout your body, your lungs breathe in our wonderful fresh air, if your bowel and bladder function, you are truly blessed. Say thank you to your healthy breasts, see them as always healthy. Close your eyes for a few seconds and imagine a life of darkness, if you are blessed with vision, be grateful. Yes, you may have pains and aches - perhaps those parts of your body are trying to tell you something. Have you ever shown them love or do you complain of how painful they are?

When you can become fully accepting of yourself, you will not fear judgement of others. You will only feel confidence when you enter a room, you will feel equal as opposed to less than. You will be able to freely share your body with your partner and enjoy your intimacy more.

My butt is too big.

My breasts are sagging.

My stomach is fat.

My legs are like tree trunks.

I can't bare to look at myself.

I am disgusted with my body.

My nose is bent.

My ears are enormous.

I've no chin.

I've a double chin.

I've bingo wings. (*Under arm loose skin*)

My skin is horrible.

You might think this is what a teenage girl would say, but no, these are all affirmations I have heard from adult women. If you are the mother of young girls, quite possibly you have told them they are beautiful and not to be comparing themselves with other girls or females in magazines. As a mother; what have you been saying to yourself? We can't expect our young ladies to grow up loving themselves and have confidence if we are constantly saying, "Do as I say not as I do!" It doesn't work like that. Your children pick up on everything you show them, whether you believe they are observing or not, it rubs off on them. Perhaps today bring awareness to what you are saying to yourself, it's never too late to change. Don't live a life of regret, let go of hoping for a better past and wishing you had loved yourself more. Do it NOW because this day will soon become your past.

Question: What traits do you find attractive in a partner? *Below are the top traits.*

- Self love
- Smile
- Confidence
- Intelligence (nothing to do with the academic results you may or may not have achieved)
- Passion
- Honesty
- Fun/Sense of Humour

Question: What traits have turned you off a partner in the past?

- Nagging
- Needy
- Seeking reassurance
- Greed
- Laziness
- Trust Issues

- Gossiping
- Very little drive or passion for themselves or for life

All energy, but vibrating on different frequencies. Men desire high vibrational partners. Just because your energy may be vibrating on a higher level, it doesn't make you a better person. We are all equal, it is your conditioning and what you believe to be true about yourself that determines what vibration you transmit on. I am sure the same goes for women and what they desire in a partner. What would the most and least attractive traits in a partner be? Quite likely you will want to attract someone with a high vibration. Regardless of what you desire, by the universal laws you will only attract back to you the same frequency you are vibrating on yourself. So be the change you wish to see. If you want a high vibrational partner, be that first for yourself. If you want to be loved, BE LOVE. If you want to attract fun, BE FUN. If you want to attract confidence, BE CONFIDENCE.

If you are vibrating on a lower frequency, not having much love for yourself, feeling depressed, feeling guilty, feeling angry, believing that nothing is going right in your life and you think that attracting a male into your life will make things better, perhaps think again. UNLESS you would like more of the feeling that you need love which may see you turn into a people pleaser to receive people's love, feeling inadequate and having someone else's company that sees the world as an unjust and unfair place to be (pain attracts pain); for some, they are very happy in misery.

And you may think that you have love for yourself by how you treat others, how you look after your children, how you help your work mates, but ask yourself these questions:

- Do I find it difficult to say no?
- Do I feel guilty if I'm not there for my children all the time?
- Do I feel like an awful person if I decide to take time of for myself?
- Do I resent my partner having his/her time?

If you can answer yes, then there is little to no self love. You have an abundance of care for others but you don't feel important enough to show that care and love to yourself. Who am I to love myself?

If you can make time each day to connect to that beauty in you, if you can thank yourself for the wonderful person you are, if you can give gratitude each day and if you can at least be willing to start to learn to love yourself, that's when the vibration shifts. That's when your frequency starts attracting new and exciting events, situations and people into your life. This is where you feel life, this is where you feel alive. Connection to self is a must, if you can't connect with yourself why be disappointed when others can't connect with you? Why feel angry when your partner has no time to talk with you? Why be resentful when your partner would rather spend time with their mates? If you can't give yourself time, love, compassion and care, your outside world will reflect the exact same back to you. If you want change, you have to be the change, not anyone else. If you cannot connect with yourself, how can you give your whole, your all in a relationship? You are only giving a portion of yourself and expecting your partner to complete you. No one can complete you except you. You are complete, you just need to love yourself enough to have time out and remember the truth of what you really are. What you really are goes beyond the human mind, it goes beyond the physical to the non-physical. You are a beautiful spiritual being having human experiences.

I received a message from a lady in her late fifties. She told me that she was depressed because she was in a loveless marriage. Her children had grown up and left the family home, her husband never told her he loved her, he never bought her a gift, even at Christmas, and he never took her out anywhere. She believed that if her husband changed she would surely change and the depression would leave. As I said before, life reflects back to you what you believe to be true about yourself. I asked the lady when was the last time she looked in the mirror and said to herself, "I Love You?" When was the last time she bought herself a gift? When was the last time she took herself out for a drive or a day out? She didn't reply to any of the questions. She only knew what she had become, the mother and the wife. When we are attached to that which we believe we are, who are we when we aren't fulfilling that role? Dedicating her life to rearing a family and taking no time to love or honour herself - sure that would be a selfish act, NOT! Sometimes married couples become total strangers because children take priority and when they leave the family home, what have they left in common? Will you remember who you are? Any loss of connection is a loss of power. A loose terminal on a car battery, the car doesn't work. A loose wire on a plug, the kettle won't boil. Connection must begin with self.

So now we have connection sorted lets move onto communication.

I believe it was the book '*Men are from Mars, Women are from Venus*' where I saw the difference between 'would' and 'could'. To me, these words sounded the exact same. I never thought too much about them, but to a man they are very different. I asked a female client to test out these words with her partner and then ask him what they felt like to him. With the word 'could' he felt she was telling him what to do, but with the word 'would' he felt she was asking him. Telling and Asking. "Could you collect the children from school?" "Would you collect the children from school?" "Could you make the dinner today?" "Would you make the dinner today?" It's always worth a try - exchange your could(s) for would(s). The ruin of many a relationship is the failure to communicate effectively. Open and honest, listen and speak.

One of the biggest, if not the all time misinterpretation of communication, are text messages. You may send a message meaning and feeling a certain way, but the receiver reads it and feels entirely the opposite way. The art of conversation in this era has dwindled down to fingers on a keypad. Can you imagine if you could see text messages flying about in the atmosphere, I don't think we would ever see sunlight, it's constant, never stops, twenty four hours a day, seven days a week. I wonder what happens in the atmosphere when you hit send from your mobile device to it arriving instantaneously on the recipient's? Where did the joke go wrong? How did the other person think I was angry? My belief is that it depends heavily upon how the receiver is feeling. Both parties are the sender and the receiver. Here's an example. A lady and man had a slight disagreement before they both went to work. She stewed over the words that he had said but decided to let them go and try to make amends by preparing a nice meal that evening.

Lady: Hi, what do you want for dinner?

Man: Whatever.

Put yourself in both positions. If you are the man and you too have stewed over the departing words from the morning, how would you read the lady's message? Is it a message that says I would like to do something nice for you or would you read it that she is still angry from earlier?

Do the same from the lady's point of view. Would you read his reply as, it's up to you, whatever you chose will be good or I don't really care, I can't be bothered telling you what I want because I'm still angry.

Have you misinterpreted a text message depending upon the mood you are in when you receive it? If I can offer one small piece of advice, never text in haste, never text when you are upset or angry because once it's gone there is no pulling it back. If you decide to text in anger be prepared for a similar one in return. What was the first text message you sent today? What was the first text message you read today? Did you send best wishes and wish the other person a wonderful day? Did you receive a message that left you with a smile? Did you send your message without any expectation of receiving one in return, you just sent it because you wanted to?

I received a message from a lady asking if I could help her with a new relationship she was in. She said he always sends a text message and ends it with a kiss emoji. For anyone who is not familiar with emojis, it's a little yellow face with a heart representing a kiss from the mouth. However, on this one occasion he did not finish his text message with the kiss emoji and automatically her thoughts went into overdrive, so much so she told me about her past relationships, how many times the men had cheated on her and she thought this time it would be different. Is this what we as humans have come to? It will be the first thing that will drive a wedge in any relationship, overthinking, did he, did she, what if, not again, I hate him, I love him, I hate her, I love her. Have we to send a message in a certain way to keep our partner feeling safe and loved? The truth of it all, no matter how you communicate it, is what you believe to be true about yourself will always manifest in your life. If that lady has old thoughts drifting about in her subconscious of previous men cheating on her, it surely will continue. She is the one that needs to communicate with herself. She needs to bring love to herself, not one thing from the outside will ever do that for any of us. Undoubtedly, a new relationship will make us feel a certain way for a period of time but when the text messages don't arrive how we expect them to, we are brought to a different feeling. If you can't fully accept and love yourself, if you find it difficult to let go of the past and old hurts, it will continually keep showing up in your life. Ultimately the communication must be with you and that divine being you are. Look in the mirror, communicate with the person looking back, tell her/him how blessed you are, tell him/her that you love them, start to feel it, start to believe it OR carry on the rest of your life needing a kiss emoji to make you feel wanted and loved. The renowned spiritual and shamanic author Don Miguel Ruiz, captures this beautifully in his book, The Four Agreements, "Speak with integrity. Say what you mean. Avoid using the word to speak against yourself or to gossip about others. Use the power of your word in the direction of truth and love. When you are immune to the opinions and actions of others, you won't be the victim of needless suffering. Find the courage to ask questions and to express what you really want. Communicate with others as clearly as you can to avoid misunderstandings, sadness and drama."

CHAPTER 9 - IT'S THE SIMPLE THINGS

Buckle up ladies! We could not have a woman's journey without a bit of romance. I am laughing at the thought that perhaps one day I will record this book for Audible. I imagine my studio man may have to leave the building until I work my way through this chapter. All of the chapters are very special to me. Each and every lady who had the courage to share their story and to trust in me, I say thank you so much. To the very beautiful, poetic lady who effortlessly shared the following story with me, oh my goodness, what can I say? It is beautiful, it is warmth, it is passion, it is freedom, it is togetherness, it is love.

Have you ever had an experience where you felt you had been transported back in time? It is an honour to share this woman's journey of love, youth, presence, gratitude, connection and communication. If you can bring awareness to the simple things in life, if you can find peace within yourself, if you can feel fully alive and feel you are connected to all, it is the most beautiful relationship to have. To find that same connection with another human form is heaven.

Timeless love, a love they felt could never be accepted by others, it would be easier for everyone if they went on their separate journeys. Many years passed by, neither found love with anyone else. From time to time they would communicate but with the passing years the communication became less and less. I believe there is no such thing as coincidence, it is what it is, everything is divinely orchestrated, as was the case when their paths crossed once more. They decided on an evening walk through rugged woodland. She said there was something magical and mystical by the untouched surrounding landscape. Pathways reminded her of when she was a very young girl at her grandfather's home. She remembered the feeling of exciting adventure among the pathways, she felt she was among the fairies once more - the smell, the views, the peace. Now in her fifties, she had been transported back to the freedom of that ten year old girl. Still very aware of where she presently was, her heart sang as she watched the sun set behind the distant hill. Standing beside her, she felt he was the gate keeper of this mystical place, giving her the gift of time past. He was as rugged and wild as the surroundings, he was at peace. As she looked, she described him as being "all man", if she was in need of shelter in this wild land she knew he would build it, he would provide for her from the land, she was safe in his presence. It was simple, it was nature, it was connection, it was effortless love. She wanted to show her independence, not asking for assistance for the steep climbs, but he had a knowing to offer his hand and help her. Returning to his home, they sat chatting over a cup of tea at the kitchen table, effortless, no expectations, no requirements, it just was and they were just BEing. As the cool of the evening approached, the woodland provided the warmth for the home. Saffron flames bounced off the walls, no other light required except that from a few flickering candles. Both stretched across the cushioned seat, conversation flowed and even when there was silence it was perfect. Communication, connection, belonging, peace, they needed for nothing else. She wanted to hold him, but being an independent woman she felt it wasn't her place. She didn't have to wait to long. As the saying goes, "Be careful what you wish for, you just might get it." He asked if it was alright by her if they kissed.

I melted when I heard this part of her story. I could have stayed in this moment with her, I could only imagine after all of those years what that moment felt like for them both.

Two naked bodies now stood by the fire light embracing one another. Everything flowed. She absorbed every touch, his smell, his shape, his sound. Time stood still. A love that can never be broken, no matter how much they tried to deny it. The energy, the light within would always draw them back together. Beautiful moments shared, unconditional love, kissing, touching, exploring, caressing, affection, what a blessing this night was. Time was neither here nor there, two bodies sweating as they loved every inch of each other. The two had connected in that very special place of divinity, a beautiful act of oneness and love. This love did not require wedding rings or vows, it did not require a birthday or anniversary for celebration, it required nothing only all that they had been gifted for free, they gave themselves freely to one another.

With no requirements or demands or expectations, they both went their separate ways once more. They allow whatever the future holds in store to unfold in its own time. She finished by saying, "I don't want people to be sad when they read this chapter because sometimes people find it difficult to understand why two people wouldn't be together if they truly loved one another." All she asked is that people see the story for what it is - how easy it is to love another once you love yourself. "Many people share years together and will never experience what I experienced that night. I am truly grateful to know what love feels like."

I believe as a human race, we sometimes over complicate things. We like to pull out all the stops, fancy restaurants, expensive holidays, top notch hotels. Certainly, it is nice to be appreciated but I believe connection and love can be simple. It can never be bought, it can only be felt.

The more I see love within me for me, the more I see love for all that dwells outside of me.

The more I find peace within me, the more I find peace within others.

Memories are being created this very second. What memories will you create today? When tomorrow arrives, today will be your timeless past.

CHAPTER 10 - THE DREAM

Many times I have asked the women I work with, "What is your dream?" Many times I hear the same reply, "I don't know." In fact, many believe they never even had a dream to begin with. If I had been asked the same question when I was at my lowest, my answer would have been, "I have no dream other than to be happy." My dream was to awaken in the morning feeling happy. Just recently I came across old diaries from 2012. I wish I could have reached back to that woman, hold her in my arms and tell her everything was going to be more than fine. I finished each diary entry with, "Please God, let tomorrow be a better day." It was an emotional read but stood to remind me why I do what I do. When I was writing my first book, A Life You Want, I had no idea how it would get published or how much money it would all cost. But one vision I had before I closed my eyes happily at night was that somewhere, someone was praying to God that tomorrow would be a better day. I repeated over and over, "Hold on, please hold on. The book is on its way." That was all I needed to keep me writing as I affirmed that the right people would come along at the right time, at an affordable price, allowing the book to be published. That is exactly what happened. When people ask, "How are your books doing?" I always reply, "They are doing what they are meant to be doing." I'm sure it's not the answer people want to hear, perhaps it is sales or numbers they want. But for me, to receive a message from a woman telling me that for the first time she went off to sleep and felt at peace, it was worth its weight in gold.

I know in my life I was not happy, no matter how hard I searched I could never find it. I did realise that in order for me to find happiness I had to make changes, big changes, scary changes. Even when I made the changes, yes there was a sense of relief, but many days I still wakened in the morning and did not feel happy, in fact, I felt pretty miserable. If this is what you are experiencing, may I bring you hope to where mine and many other women's lives have brought them. The truth is I AM Peace. I AM Love. When you make the decision to begin to love yourself it will be the best decision you will ever make in your life. The time will come when you have had enough of the experiences you are going through and yes, it will terrify you to make the change, but rest easy because it is just your mind telling you that you are moving into unfamiliar territory. Looking back, and in such a short space of time, so many amazing experiences have happened in my life and they happened because I said yes to me. I said yes to what my heart was guiding me to do. I had no clue where my life would lead me and am still pretty clueless as to what will happen for the rest of it but for now, and in this present moment, I choose to be happy. I believe when you step into your power and truth, you give many more the permission to step into theirs. When I say power I don't mean control of others. I mean your divine magnificence which continues to unfold effortlessly every day. All you have to do is take a look in the mirror, look into your eyes, see the reflection looking back at you and give yourself permission to remember that you are so amazing. If you only knew what your were capable of, if I told you now what you were capable of, you wouldn't believe me because there is no way on this earth I would have believed anyone if they told me what they saw in me. That's why life is a blessing, let it unfold in its own time. You have to start letting go of old hurts, resentments, blaming others for your situation, being the people pleaser. None of these serve you at all. If something does not feel good, it's not for you. Step away or let it go, don't be afraid, affirm I AM SAFE.

One day it will all fall into place, it is you that will make this happen, the most amazing people will appear and events will start to unfold so watch out for them!

I have an endless list of wonderful people I have had the honour to cross paths with. My first two books have assisted so many to create new lives. My hope for this book is that it will inspire you to take back your power, create the life you desire and be at peace. My wish is for everyone to experience joy, love, laughter, peace and many blessings. You have the exact same within you that I have within me, we have originated from the same source energy, there is nothing to separate us except our thoughts. What would you like to do? How would you like to feel? All is waiting for you. It has always been there just waiting for you to give yourself permission. My dreams unfold everyday, I don't see them as dreams anymore, I just see them as part of my life experiences. I AM Peace, I AM Love, I AM so very Grateful.

CHAPTER 11 - WHO ARE YOU NOT TO BE....

" " Who are you not to be greatness?" Words spoken to me by one of the most humble men I have been blessed to know. The same man said, "You are the host to the God divine energy." My road map, my clarity, my knowing. Declan Coyle, author of The Green Platform, has listened to my laughs, has saw my tears and he saw within me something I could not see in myself. As I sat in front of him sobbing, telling him I felt false rehearsing for an upcoming event, he looked at me and said "Evelyn, who are you not to be greatness?" So to you the reader I say the same, "Who are you not to be greatness?" Who are you not to walk into a room with your head high and shoulders back? Who are you not to speak with people first? Who are you not to go for that dream job? Who are you not to ask questions? Who are you not to be with the person you love? Who are you not to speak your truth? Who are you not to show your talents and skills? Who are you not to have a monetary exchange for your services?

Who are you not to wear your best dress? Who are you not to be greater than yesterday?

When you stand in your greatness, you inspire others to do the same. When you smile, you give others permission to do so . When you speak your truth, you give many the courage to speak theirs. Someone has to go first, if we all stand back and wait, the dance floor will always be empty. Let us rise together. Let us support each other. Let us help create the dreams for each other. Let us be the light and love that will shower this earth. There is no ego in your greatness, you will still be the same person, except you will be your greatest version. Can you bring your greatness to this day? Can you bring joy and laughter to this day? Can you bring hope to this day? You must be the change and in doing so, you bring the change to your outside world. This is how effortless change is. Whatever you wish to see transpire in your lifetime, it starts with you. Yes, you! No one is responsible for your change, you make that choice.

Who are you not to be greatness? Thank you Declan for believing in me, sometimes that's all it takes. I think it's absolutely fabulous that you are in all three of my books!

Chapter 12 - Beginning the Change

I wish to share this chapter for those who may be asking themselves, "Where do I even begin?"

A wonderful lady came to me because she was now ready for change but she had no idea where or how to begin. She didn't have any big dream of what her life was to look like but she was very clear that she couldn't go on feeling the way she was feeling. She was very honest that she couldn't look at herself in the mirror, she really didn't like much about herself. Being a business woman for many years she had employees, she had built her business up from nothing but with all of the time she gave to her business, she had little time for her family. She was earning less money than her staff and most certainly had no time for herself. When businesses had to close in 2020 due to COVID, she had to let her employees go and declare bankruptcy. In one way it was a relief that she didn't have to waken each day to an unfulfilling job but on the other side, she felt guilt for others not having a job to go to and a fear that she also needed to earn money.

Every morning she woke up exhausted, she had no excitement, no love, no joy. She began by practicing gratitude, giving thanks for all that she had, she felt impatient - why wasn't she feeling the words she was saying? Many can relate to this, we say thank you for this and thank you for that but with no real feeling and sometimes it takes for us to lose many material possessions in our lives, sometimes it takes for us to lose people in our lives, sometimes it takes for us to fall into ill health before we truly see what we had to be grateful for. I never wanted this lady to wait until her body fell into ill health before she started to love it, I never wanted her to loose her eyesight before she started to appreciate the beauty that she was and the beauty that surrounded her. What I wanted was irrelevant - this was entirely her choice. I asked if the people she was surrounded by each day were happy at their work, she said no. I asked if there were couples in her life that were happy in their relationships, she said no. Your vibe attracts your tribe and this does not make people better or worse than others, they are who they are and that's perfectly okay but when you are surrounded with people who are generally unhappy in life, why would you be any different? Why would you want to be the odd one out because undoubtedly, this would take you out of the 'normal' category. The key to any change is to get back to loving yourself, or in a lot of cases, starting to love yourself. Do not wait on the right job to come along to be happy, do not wait on the perfect partner to arrive at your door to be happy, do not wait on your bank to be full of money to be happy, it is not how true happiness is achieved. Start by breaking old habits, start by bringing in positive change. Start by bringing awareness to the words you are speaking to yourself, try to speak kindly to yourself a few times each day.

The lady had two little dogs. She would feel guilty if she didn't get to walk them during the daytime, but with the exhaustion each morning and the downward spiral of thoughts and emotions, it was a chore to walk. HOWEVER, she made a promise to herself to rise at 6am each morning and begin to walk. I have to mention that this lady is only at the beginning of her change, but now she has other ladies of the same mindset to help her along the way. She is beginning to realise that people do think and act differently, people can be happy awaking each morning, enjoying their job and people can be happy in relationships. Be happy within and watch how everything changes around you. Below are the words the lady sent after her first morning of starting a new habit:

Morning...I just want to share how my morning went. I feel so happy. Today I felt a shift. I spoke with Evelyn yesterday and set a goal to get up early and walk my dogs. I woke at 6am....that's normally the middle of the night to me. I got up and out with my little dogs. I also received a beautiful voice message from one of the ladies on our group...thank you. It was such a lovely walk . So peaceful with the birds singing and the river flowing beside me. That was the first time in a long time I could honestly say I felt peace and contentment in myself. It actually made me emotional in a good way. I felt great when I got home. My daughter woke not long after and said she wanted to start her day positively and said she was going for a run. Out of nowhere I just decided I would love to go and run. I haven't ran in years. Off we went to the beach. I ran along the beach and all the time I was thanking my feet and legs for carrying me, my heart and lungs for pumping the blood and oxygen around my body to help me breathe, my ears for enabling me to hear my music and my inner voice for telling me, "You can do this, keep going." I'm buzzing this morning. Thank you.

In an essay by David Everett in *The Colombian Orator, 1797,* he wrote, "Large streams from little fountains flow, Tall oaks from little acorns grow."

- Remember to remember who you are
- Take time each day for yourself
- Begin speaking kindly to yourself
- Get out of the comfy clothes and the "sure no one will see me" attitude and dress for you
- Rise earlier, morning time is so precious
- Get excited with the unknown
- Set a challenge for yourself
- Accept yourself
- Start forming new habits
- Be the change you wish to see unfold in your life

I recorded this chapter in audio and sent it to the lady. When I send stories back this way, a lot of the time the women see their story entirely differently. It is very emotional for people. Sometimes, what we see in others we fail to see in ourselves, and sometimes we fail to see in ourselves what others see in us.

"Wow.....that brought tears to my eyes. To hear someone describe my feelings and my life back to me like that has made me realise how much I was just existing for so long. If someone else was talking to me like that about how they felt about life, I would be heartbroken for them so why did I let it go on for so long? I already feel miles away from who that person was and I know things will just continue to get better. I'm so excited about my future."

CHAPTER 13 - THE WARRIOR

I am the youngest of five siblings. I was born in 1973 in Dublin. My mother was a wonderful woman and did her best for us, although she suffered with anxiety and depression all her life.

My father was an alcoholic and this resulted in a very traumatic childhood. I grew up a fearful child with low self-confidence and lack of self-esteem.

When I was nine years old my eldest brother died of a heart attack. He was my rock and as a little girl I idolised him. He was the protective father figure as my own father could be extremely cruel and abusive at times.

I struggled at school and left at fifteen with no formal qualifications. At sixteen I fell pregnant with my son and again struggled greatly. I definitely did not have the maturity or life skills required to be a mother. I went from job to job and was never confident in myself or my abilities.

At twenty one I met my future husband and finally felt like I had some security. When I think back now, I was desperate for someone to "make me happy" which obviously I now understand is never the answer as it can only be found within.

We bought a house together and we began our sixteen year relationship. My husband came to the relationship with his own troubles, depression, and alcohol issues.

I continued to struggle with my own mental health throughout the marriage and when I was twenty three my mother passed away with cancer. I was beyond heartbroken as she had always been a support to me with my son.

My depression ebbed and flowed for years, I never sought any help with it, just battled on struggling through life.

After my mother passed away, I cut off contact with my father, only seeing him again when he was terminally ill to help my sisters nurse him at home. This was very difficult as he remained abusive and difficult up to the end.

My marriage began to fall apart and we eventually split up. I was lost and riddled with guilt that my marriage had failed. The year my marriage ended, my second brother took his own life. This had a devastating effect on the family. I would say my darkest days followed as I was consumed with grief and spiralled into a crippling depression.

My son was away to college at this point and I found myself alone in an apartment, working full-time in a job I didn't enjoy, drinking too much wine alone. I was basically a broken human. My friends did their best to help me and I eventually managed to get myself back on my feet although I was still unhappy and also very lonely.

About eight months after my marriage ended I met a guy on a night out with friends and embarked on a whirlwind relationship with him. He lived in Belfast, approximately one hundred miles from my home. I spent the next few months travelling up and down to see him, until eventually I decided to quit my unloved job, leave my apartment and relocate to be with him. But I am sure if you are on any kind of a journey, you will know that unless you fully love the person staring back at you in the mirror, you will never receive love from anything or anyone on the outside. I desperately wanted to be loved, I didn't believe or even know that I could learn to love myself. I searched to find love in everything outside of me. Unfortunately I could only attract back to me the same vibration I was on myself. Sometimes we might think, "If I only knew then what I know now," but such are our journeys, no matter how difficult they feel at the time.

When I look back, all the signs were there, red flags flying. However, I ignored them all and seen the relationship as a chance to start over in a new city and escape, to basically run away. The relationship continued for eight years and during this time it became more and more dysfunctional and abusive. I found myself living in a nightmare. I was constantly scared and felt totally trapped. I didn't tell my family or friends the extent of the abuse as I was so ashamed for staying. My anxiety was at an all time high and the depression was ever present. Things became so bad that I did contemplate suicide, but the thoughts of what this would do to my son stopped me as I already knew the impact suicide brings.

I reached a point one day where I thought, "I cannot let this continue, I don't want this life, this nightmare, to go on anymore." I went to see my doctor and she put me on anti-depressants and anxiety medicine. I did not tell her about the abusive relationship I was in because I was ashamed. I desperately wanted to change my circumstances, but I didn't know how. I was working full-time through all of this and knew that there was an employee assistant programme I could access. I made the decision to contact them. I did not disclose the abusive relationship to them either but I did talk about my mental health and requested access to help through their counselling services.

This was the beginning of change for me. I was forty six.

I began weekly therapy sessions with an amazing lady, I started to really work through my past. I embraced the advice she gave me and started to see the benefits of my hard work. However, I was still in the abusive relationship but as the weeks passed, I became stronger in myself and I made the decision to leave. I did not know how I would do this, as I had no financial security, the house was not in my name and I was petrified. However, the thought of staying the same became more painful than the fear of leaving and after yet another cycle of abuse I decided to go.

I have a dog and he's my best friend, he had protected me and kept me safe at times during the relationship and I couldn't and wouldn't leave him behind as my ex-partner had threatened to hurt him in the past. So I did not want to accept the offer of sheltered accommodation as this would mean leaving my beloved dog behind or in a shelter.

I searched online for private property to rent, but knew I didn't have enough money for a deposit and one month's rent up front and knew I would have to leave in secret, with just my bare essentials. I saw a little cottage to rent outside of Belfast and called the landlord. I was so desperate at this point that I prayed for help. I will never forget that moment. I was sat in my car with my dog on the side of the road. The landlord was a lovely man and he asked me to come view the house that evening. I met with himself and his wonderful wife later that day. It was perfect and they were happy to accept my dog. It was unfurnished and needed some work done. I explained my situation, how I couldn't afford to pay all at that time but they kindly suggested that I pay the deposit and the rent over three months. My prayers had been answered, I was overwhelmed and relieved. I then called my sisters. This was the first time I had ever told them the extent of the abuse and what I was living with, it was a very, very emotional day! The next day, while my ex-partner was at work, I packed up my life in black bags, I filled the car, took my dog and I closed the door for the last time. I drove the one hundred miles to my sister's home and stayed with her for one week until I got the keys to my new home. I had nothing, zero furniture, not even a duvet. My friends and family all helped me. I was finally home.

Since then, my positive journey has continued. I love my little safe haven, I love my life, my freedom, my family, my friends and of course my four legged companion is still by my side!

I am out enjoying my photography again, something which I have always found brings me peace and joy. I also love crafts and again, my creativity has bloomed. My journey back to myself has begun.

I have so many plans for 2021 and finally feel like I know who I am and I love me! I am now looking to change my job as I've always wanted to go back to work in care. I'm excited for my new life and will be forever thankful, grateful and humbled by the support I've received which has helped me come this far. I started taking yoga classes when I first began to see the counsellor. I still practice now, the deep breath exercises are great for calming me when I feel anxious but it has subsided greatly now. I listen to a lot of mindfulness tutorials and follow what Evelyn talks about.

I walk a lot, I just love being out in nature, in the woods, by the sea etc. I've always loved being outdoors, but for a long time I would go for long walks, and not actually be there. I would physically be there, but my thoughts were always racing, so much so, I could not tell one thing I'd seen or even which route I took, because I was seldom present. Now when I walk, I look at the colours, the absolute beauty around me, the wildlife and listen to the sounds. I love myself and I love my life. I do not seek it in anyone or anything. Every day I open my back door and say thank you for the day, for my health, my family and affirm that I will have a wonderful day. I tell myself to always trust the process even when I feel worried or anxious.

One of my favourite quotes, from Sarah Beth McClure, has kept me moving forward, "Though you may hold your sword in a shaky hand, I see the dragons you are slaying, carry on warrior, you are stronger than you know."

Chapter 14 - The Ending or Beginning? It's Your Choice

You can look on this chapter in one of two ways, is it the ending, or is it the beginning? It is the ending of this book, but could it be the beginning of your chapter?

We all have experiences in this life and you may or may not relate to some of the stories. You may have an entirely different story but none the less, the feelings and emotions you experience are the same as everyone else. Sometimes the harder people fall, the stronger they rise. Sometimes it takes the same experience to recur over and over and over before you wake up. Sometimes it takes you to lose a loved one before you feel gratitude in your life. Sometimes it takes that one last insult before you make the change. Sometimes it takes you to be on the edge of ending it all before you decide you want to live. I never want any of these experiences for people, but sometimes this is what has to happen in order for you to take responsibility and change. Sometimes people are happy in their misery because it's a familiar feeling, because they have lots of people around them feeling the same, because if they remain a victim to the outside circumstance, it removes them from having to take any responsibility.

I do not advocate abuse of any form and NO, you are not deserving of any of it. NO, it is not your fault......so if it's not your fault, why have you to take responsibility?

If you only see yourself as the man or woman that you are, only a body moving through this life, then chances are you will give your power away to everything outside of you. If, however, you can begin to recognise that there is so much more to you than your physical appearance, even for just a few seconds, then this is the beginning of your chapter.

Are you waiting on the new job? Are you waiting on the new partner? Are you waiting on the new body? Are you waiting on the weather to change? Are you waiting on Covid to go away? Are you waiting on your mother's permission? Are you waiting on your father's permission? Are you waiting for your partner to agree with you?

If you are waiting on that perfect moment or perfect body or perfect partner or perfect bank balance, you will always be waiting. How about thinking instead that it's all waiting for you? It is sitting waiting for you to make the change. It's waiting for you to stop waiting. It's all sitting there for you to say YES YES YES, I AM DESERVING, I AM WORTHY, I AM READY. What are you willing to do today to make that change? Watch out for those thoughts that will come in:

- It's alright for him/her, they don't know my story
- Don't be getting out of bed, it's far too early
- You aren't feeling what you are saying
- These things never happen for the likes of you
- Wait until someone else does it first

Remember, by the time you are thirty five years of age, there is ninety five percent of you already conditioned. You probably just go into auto-pilot mode when reacting to a situation. It just is what it is, you've been conditioned by everything that surrounded you. Your parents, your teachers, the news, your friends, your religious leaders, your government and society. I will always give people the benefit of the doubt and affirm, "forgive them for they know not what they do." People have said or done things to you in the past, just like you when you have reacted to situations. You possibly said words in the heat of the moment and truthfully you have no idea the lasting effect those words have had. Someone has done that to you in the past but it's stuck with you, it became part of what you believed to be true about yourself. On the upside, there is still five percent willing and wanting for you to remember, there is still a good fighting chance that life can be different. Can you imagine if these two percentages where in a boxing ring, ninety five versus five, who would you place your money on? Remember, when you start to make change, when you start to fight to love yourself, that ninety five is not going to go quietly into the night. BUT, if you are consistent and persistent, that five percent will grow and grow and grow. There will come a time when the roles are reversed and the really good news is that you won't have to wait thirty five years. In your thirty five years you were unaware, unawakened as to what was happening, but now with what you know to be true, take back that power. YOU ARE THE MASTER. I AM THE MASTER. People are in search of instant gratification; when we order something online, it arrives in a matter of days but life and energy doesn't work like this. When you initially start making changes, it must become a daily habit. You must start letting go of the things that do not serve you and start bringing in good daily habits and when you want to quit, DON'T, because it will be harder the next time round. I welcome challenges, through challenges we grow.

So is this the ending? What will you do now? Will you say thank you for the life you have when you read other peoples stories? Will you believe that you are deserving of happiness? Will you take one action in the direction you wish to go, even though you don't know where go is? Will you start to believe that you are more than the human body you are occupying?

- Find gratitude – stop complaining
- Praise people – stop gossiping
- Love yourself – stop finding fault
- Take action – stop procrastinating
- Be the victor — stop being the victim
- Become the mentor – stop being the fixer
- Trust – stop fearing

- Bring in one new habit – let go of one habit no longer serving you
- Say yes to you – stop being the people pleaser
- Be you – stop trying to fit in
- Find joy – let go of misery
- Be free – stop being the prisoner of you own thoughts

This life is a gift. Eight years ago when I went to a charity to ask for money to warm my home, when I had to borrow a few hundred pounds to buy a car, if you had told me I would write three books, I would be speaking to people all over the world , I would be rising every morning full of excitement for each day, I would be travelling abroad many times throughout the year, lock down or no lock down, I would never have believed it. Most importantly, if someone had told me you will love yourself unconditionally, you will be at peace and you will only see joy for the life you have, I think I would have fallen to my knees and broke down because that's all I ever wanted. I just wanted to be happy in myself and I was prepared to do whatever it took to find that. If my ego comes in and tells me I can't do something, I say, "Just you watch me!" So to my wonderful ego I say thank you because you know exactly what to say in order to help me grow. Lock down or no lock down, pandemic or no pandemic, it's life or death and I choose life. I choose to live every second of every day, to bring joy to my life and the lives of others. Together we are stronger, together we are better, together we reconnect our truth, our souls, our spirits. Together we raise the vibrations of this beautiful earth and not one thing will stand in our way.

Love & Light

Evelyn. x

EVELYN MCALEER

Printed in Great Britain
by Amazon